HONEYSUCKLE AND FORGIVENESS

by Jessie Michelle

D0168262

This is for time.

I dedicate this, not to a person, but to a time. To a time when I once saw in myself everything that I wished I could be. And to a time when I know that I will once again see it.

I dedicate this to the time it takes to teach myself my worth.

And to the time I hope you are setting aside to discover yours.

TABLE OF CONTENTS

HONEYSUCKLE AND FORGIVENESS

HONEYSUCKLE AND FORGIVENESS

I bathe in honeysuckle
and forgiveness.
One for my skin
and one for my soul.
I drench myself
head to toe
with the words
that I've been longing
to hear.
I have forgiven others.
Thrown to the wind
any baggage
that I have been carrying
on this walk that I call life.
But the thing I can't quite seem
to conquer is my mind.
This fear,
this uneasiness,
this anger;
it is deep-rooted.
I try to pluck it from the ground.
Like a weed
it has been stealing the life
from right beneath me.
But at the same time,
like everything
that stems from the earth,

there is still some beauty
to be found inside.
I let the tears fall.
They flood the earth
as if an arc was on its way.
Drowning everything
I denied access aboard me.
It is time.
There are things
that need to be left behind.
Things that I have let
weigh me down
for far too long.
And while I know that
I am not alone,
this storm creates an ocean
that no one seems
to want to cross.
So here I am.
An island
so far deep out to sea
that I have only myself to rely on.
But then I remember...

I am my own safety net.
I will once again meet the shore
even if I have to swim alone.

WASTED

I am empty. Wasted.
Not the kind of wasted
that occupies your Friday night.
But the wasted you hide
from your lover.
The wasted you hide
from everyone.

I am wilting away.
Minute by minute,
a little piece of me dies down.
But I know
that there is hope on the horizon.

I can almost taste the victory
of overcoming the storm.
The waves are strong,
and some days, still pull me under.

Never long enough to drown me.
Just long enough to
remind me that there is still
a war to fight.

SEAMS

I am not the same
woman I used to be.
My canvas is no longer
blank.
It is covered in
stories.
There are cracks
woven throughout
my spine.
Ripped pages
and tattered seams.

Am I broken?

Or, am I shedding
all that needs to be
left behind?

Some say
that I have fallen apart.
I say that
I am finally
coming together.

WALLS

I am building walls.
And not the kind
that are meant to be torn down.
The kind that are
meant to trap inside
all that I too easily give away.
The kind of walls
that I am free to open and shut
as my soul needs.
They protect but never
suffocate me.
The kind of walls that
I am only
now learning exist.
I am building walls.
Not to keep people out.

I am building walls
to keep myself in.

CHAINS

Shadows dance in my mind.
I am reminded of
a time in which *I* once
belonged to *me*.

I have become a prisoner
of my ~~thoughts~~ fears.
Barricaded behind
a wall of my own creation.

I am slowly plucking them
from my mind,
like the vicious weeds they are.
They threaten to steal
the life right out beneath me.
But I have found
strength in the wreckage
that has become my soul.

And I will continue
to toss aside anything
that dreams of chaining me down.

EVOLVE

I am changing. Evolving.
I barely recognize
the face in the mirror,
let alone the voices in my head.

I am not the woman
I imagined I would become.
And somehow,
I am ~~satisfied~~ proud of that.

My reflection speaks nothing
of the faults
I replay in my mind.

I am a woman.
A curved,
silent,
screaming woman.

And today,
that is all I need to be.

TIGHT

I clenched my fist tight.
Closed my eyes
and begged my soul
to let go of everything
that I've been holding on to.

I have weighed myself down
with moments that have long passed.
With dreams that have been
replaced with nightmares.

I no longer need to carry the past.

I don't need to know
what tomorrow will bring.
I just need to breathe.

> *To get through this moment,*
> *I need to breathe.*

BOUNCE

I bounce back.
And when I say
that I bounce back,
I don't mean
back to reality that you
have put before me.
I bounce back to a place
where my feet
rest on the ground.

A place where
the weight of my soul
is valued more
than the weight
on my soles.

I bounce back
to a place where
I just don't care.
Don't give me wrong,
I care about a lot.
But when I bounce back,
I bounce back to a place
where I find beauty in me
without you having to see it first.

HONEYSUCKLE AND FORGIVENESS

I bounce back
and maybe it's more
appropriate to say that I bounce up.

Because when I bounce back
I'm coming from a place that was so low
that heaven felt forever away.

I find that my hands are open.
They are free.
They're not looking
for anything to hold onto.
They're not looking for something
to grasp the life out of.
I bounce back
and I find myself smiling.
Not because you smiled first.
But because I smiled first.

I bounce back.

LIES

I won't die down.

I won't cower.

I won't lose my voice
so that others can be heard.

I won't drop to the ground,
so you can walk more freely.

And I promise,
I won't hate myself
if sometimes
these turn out to be lies.

DEMONS

I feel it in my chest tonight.
The silent scream. A voiceless demon.
Its tugging on my soul.

Eating away at me from the inside out.
It beats loudly for a moment.
And in the next, it disappears.

A wicked game to play on me.
It never leaves.
Just hides in the crevasses.
Hides in the cracks.

It waits for me to forget that
it once lingered in the hallow
of my chest.

And then, like a bolt of lightening,
out of nowhere,
it crashes down upon me.
Stealing the spotlight for a moment
and reminding me that even the
most powerful demons
eventually leave.

STUCK

I get stuck.
Frozen in time.
I fixate on what was
instead of what is.
I lose myself to the past
and fall so far behind
that I fear I may never
catch back up.

Maybe someday
I'll learn to be a little more
of this moment and a little less
of yesterday.

FEAR

I have housed fear
more often than I'd like to admit.
I stare it down.
Scream (in my head)
every word that comes to mind.
Praying that soon enough
my words will mean something.

But fear is a wicked beast.
She is strong. She is a survivor.
And as much as I have to force
myself to believe it,
So am I.

Fear may carry the weight of
every grain of sand in the hour glass,
but I know that time weighs more.
I am dressed in the armor of yesterday
and hope for tomorrow.
Both of which used to scare me.
But fear is a liar.
And I am learning that what was
and what will be, hold more weight
than uncertainty.

DIVE

If I asked you to measure me,
how would you do it?
Would you hold your hands
out in front of you?
Empty.
Trying to gauge just
how much of me you could
hold on to?

Or would you rip open your chest?
Pull out your
scarlet beating heart
and tell me to dive in?

Would you want to know
all of the pieces?
The ones that are
broken and
and left to sit
in ruins.
Damaged by the sunlight
and left to dry
in the same world
that promised me life.

Or do you just want
to know the painted pieces?
The ones that hang
in the gallery
for all to see.
Lights shining down
on the clean edges
and polished exterior.

Is that all there is to know?
Is it really about what you want to
know?
Or, is it about what I want to show you?
Do I give more to
this world than a filtered snapshot?
Something that can be learned with a
glance?

Or am I a story?
Carrying more than one chapter.
Am I giving this world
something to read?
Or am I simply an excerpt
that will someday be forgotten?

REMAIN

Is it possible to lose yourself
more than you find yourself?
Can you shed layer
after layer without disappearing?
I find myself in a constant state of motion.
Never pausing.
Never slowing down.
Back and forth.
Up and down.
There is no calm within me.
I hear voices swimming
around inside my head.
Screaming to be heard.
I slowly let them slip out.
One at a time.
I find myself alone with my
silent screaming.
Afraid of the layers that remain.
But even more afraid
of not discovering what is left
beneath.
And so, I stay still.
Silent.
And listen to all
that my fears
are trying to teach me.

TELL ME

I having been chasing dreams.
Running through streets
that don't seem to want to end,
I am trying to find my way
back home.

I have prayed,

> *"Please, God, give me a sign."*

I want to know when to turn left.
Tell me when to turn the lights down
and put my mind to sleep.

> *Tell me when.*
> *Tell me how.*
> *Tell me.*

LINES

I celebrate these lines.
The curves.
The body that cradles this soul.
These walls, this skin,
so much more than
a shield to protect
me from this world.
I always assumed being less would
somehow make me more.
But the more I strip away,
the less I recognize myself.

So, I will love the layers that
make me,
even when I feel that
I shouldn't.

WARS

I am at war with my heart.
My soul is fighting
to become so much more
than I thought possible.
At the same time,
the world is telling me
to shrink down
and become a little
less visible each day.
When did I learn to pay
more attention to
the growth of my body
than I did
the growth of my soul?

How did I forget that
the beauty within
me will stay even when
what lies
on the surface fades?

RACE

I will dance with
my insecurities until I learn
to outrun them.
I stay at their side.
Keep them within
an arms reach.
We will waltz until we run.
And then, we race.

HEARTACHE

I don't wear heartache like I used to.
Tears don't weigh down
upon my shoulders,
forcing me to walk low.
Head down.
Eyes to the ground.
I don't carry weights
that no longer belong to me,
memories that have been
shattered,
or love that has been lost.
I don't give myself
time to get lost in yesterday.

My soul is already full with
the hope for tomorrow.

CEMENT

I stopped looking
back on yesterday
and I almost forgot
about tomorrow.
I gave up on dreaming, on wishing.

I gave up on the thought
of something so much more.

I became cemented to this moment.
Trapped in a bottle
that I was too afraid to shatter,
I was stuck.
Running out of air
and running out of time.

FORTRESS

This body is mine.
And yet, for far too long
I have let these curves,
these lines define me.
They tell a story that has never left
my lips.
And until now, I have never tried
to stop them.

But I am building a wall.

No, a fortress.

A structure of nothing more
than the truth that lives inside me.

Not to be defined by the
curve of my smile
or my hips.
But my soul.

OFTEN

I have a tendency to
get lost in my thoughts.
I open doors and
they flood my mind.
Like the waves crashing
on the shore after the storm,
they pull me out to sea.
There is no escaping them.
And even if I was able to,
I am not sure I would want to.

I am a product of every moment
up until this one.
Every smile that stretched across my face,
every tear that watered my soul.

I am made of every moment
I have ever touched.

And I am fighting so
hard to love all of the moments
that have come together
to make me.

HOME

I find myself lost in the darkness.
From time to time,
I let myself wander behind
the shadows that I have grown
to fear.
I have to remind myself,
drill it into my head;
that there is strength in this.

Strength in the searching,
the navigating through the darkness.

I won't give up.
I may look lost,
but I just haven't found my way.

I'm still chasing the sun.
Looking for a home to call my own.

HER

I have been
hiding from myself.
Ashamed of the lines
I let define me.
I have forgotten
the beauty within.
I find myself constantly
comparing the space
I take up to those
in the world around me.

I lust after
the woman that dances
in my dreams.
Not to hold her in my arms.

No, to be her.

I imagine the layers falling
to the floor.
Losing myself and becoming
myself all in a moment.
One by one,
I become the woman
I sleep to dream of.

The woman I see through
filtered eyes.

Perfection from a distance.

She wears her lines as if
they were sewn for royalty.
Head to toe, she is
drowning in beauty.
For a moment,
I lose myself in her image
and forget who I am.
Then, as if waking from a dream,
I remember that we are made of
more than the walls
that our bones carry.

We are all the same.
Flesh and soul.
I am her.

PAUSE

I want to pause.
Not stop,
just freeze time for a minute.
Not just this moment,
I want to pause the past.
Keep it from replaying
in my mind.
Pause the future
and take away the weight
it holds.

I need to find myself in
this moment.
Free of chains.
Free of fears.
I need to find myself
free of everything
I am letting hold me down.

HAUNTED

My reflection haunts me.
It enhances my fears and magnifies
everything I wish I could change.
I stare it down,
and it laughs in my face.
I see bags and lines
that grow more prominent
by the minute.
They etch out my story without
even asking my permission.
I count flaws as if they were stars.
I pray for them to stop;
to disappear in the morning light.
But they are never ending.
They are in me. They are me.
But is that all I am?
Can I dig deeper.
Look past the story that is spelled out in
front of me and search for the truth that
is more than skin deep.
Ignore the lines that are
creeping in
and pay attention to the
ones spilling onto the page.

SKIN

There are days
I wear my insecurities
better than I do my own skin.
They are heavy and pull me down.
They taunt my soul
with lies and empty threats.
Those are the days I give myself
just a little more time
to breathe.
To find some sort of beauty
in all the weeds
that I have been hiding behind.

I search for a way
out of this maze of torment
I have built around myself.
Tossing aside all
the baggage that I have been
carrying with me.

Nothing weighs more than a soul
that is burdened with
everything but love.

GROWTH

I will break. I will crumble.
I have been known
to leave shards of my soul behind.
But, I will not throw away
the pieces
that touch the ground.
I am not a flag
that must be waved with dignity
or lowered at the sight of tragedy.

I am a spirit that wants to do
nothing more than grow.
Even if that means
I must start from the bottom.

SLEEP

For so long,
I have carried insecurities
like they have some right
to rest on my shoulders.
Like they have staked
their claim on this land that
I know to be mine.

They weigh me down.
Change me.

They tarnish my soul.
An uninvited guest,
they are known
for overstaying their welcome.
They haunt me in my dreams.
Disrupting my slumber
and keeping me from sleeping.

When I finally slept,
I would dream only
of the woman
I was longing to be.

But my soul has kicked
this unwelcome tenant out.

And my heart is now vacant.
Free to let in only welcomed visitors.

CHOICES

I have been forgotten.
My soul, abused.
My name, tarnished.
I have been pushed to the side.
Pushed to the edge.
I have been forced
to give away pieces of my soul
that I so desperately miss.

I am the demon
that sleeps beneath my bed.
I am the one that bends
and twists my reflection
in the mirror.
Contorting every truth that
I have buried
deep inside of me.
I pull at them,
so desperately trying to
wake these truths before
the fall into the trap
of tomorrow.
Before they fall into
the wrong hands;
mine.

I have become the thing
I have feared.
The voice I have tried to run from.
I have become something
I don't wish to speak of.
Something that scares me.

I am my own worst enemy.

But, now I know, I don't have to be.

MIGHTY

I have walked empty streets alone
only to be forced
to hide in the shadows.

Danced when the music
stopped playing,
because, in my mind,
the tune never stops.

I have trampled one demon
only to be suffocated by the next.
I have lost sleep to fears that
I thought I had conquered.
Fallen for dreams
that I thought would come true.

I sit in silence.
And stand tall throughout the storms.

I am strong, mighty, fierce.

Even when the world wants me to believe
I am losing myself.

RIGHTS

I have fallen victim to my own mind.
Grown afraid of the space
I occupy in this world.
Mind and body.

I fear I have taken too much.

My body changes by the day and so
does my soul.
I know it is easier to
see the curve of my hips
than it is to see the smile in my soul.

But believe me,
I am growing.
I am growing.

And I will never again be afraid
to take up the space that so
rightfully belongs to me.

FLOODS

I have a tendency
to get lost in my thoughts.
I open doors to my mind
and the words that are
swimming around, flood my mind.

Like the waves
crashing on the shore
after a storm,
they pull me out to sea.

There is no escaping them.
And if I was able to,
I am not sure
that I would want to.

I am a product of
every moment up
until this one.

Every smile
that stretched
across my face,
every tear
that has watered my soul.

I am made
of every moment
that has ever
kissed my skin.

And I have been fighting
so hard to love
all of the pieces
that have come together
to make me.

ECHO

Some days,
the night goes quiet
before you do.
Other days,
the wind howls loud enough
to sing you to sleep.

Tonight, the air is quiet.
I am once again
left with my own voice
and the echoes
that trail.

And I can't help but wonder,
where do I go from here?

LOST

Can I leave?
Run away from everything
that I promised myself
I would become?
Out of sight,
will I be out of mind too?
If I run far enough,
will I lose too much of myself
to ever fully come back?
Can I recover from the damage
that I brought upon my soul?

I don't want to pick up the ashes
and build something new.

Set my soul ablaze,
I want a rebirth.
I want to find myself in something whole.
Something greater.
I want to find myself in every place I thought
I once was lost.

CONQUER

Will I ever be more than *enough*?
I try to convince myself
that I am where I need to be.
But the constant battle
between my mind and my heart
is never ending.

Conquering or be conquered.

Some days it seems
as if there is no in between.

KNOWN

I know there is more to this life
than walking in the sunlight.
I want to be known
for traveling in
even the darkest hours of the
night.
When even my shadow has left me,
and I feel as though
I am on my own.

Let me walk tall.
Let me walk strong.
Let me walk as though the world
is watching,
but not giving a damn
what they think.

MORE

I drown in my insecurities.
Bound by the flaws
that I see in the mirror,
they overpower me.
Reflections that I wish
I could escape.

I am growing, and I know soon,
I will swim instead of drown.
I will stare at the beauty inside
without clenching my eyes shut.
I will search for all
of the pieces that I have lost.
I know they are inside.
Buried deep within me.

I am more than I tell myself.
I am more than I have let myself believe.
So much more.

TRAVELS

My body is formed
of curves.
Soft edges and supple lines.
It wasn't until I began to see
the beauty in this,
that he decided
I was a road worth traveling.

But by then,
I was already gone.
Lost on an adventure in which
I had no intention of returning from.

OPTIONS

Maybe I'll stand still
and grow tired
of the silence.

Or, maybe I'll forget
I ever wanted to leave.
We live in a world
of "maybe" and "what if".
Some days, the possibilities
can cause greatness.
The idea that we can be more.
Do more. See more.

But then,
there are the days
when the weight of options
is almost
too much to bear.
Too much to imagine.
Too much to conquer.

Do we stay silent and still?

Or take a step?
Any step.
Is moving forward the only direction
worth going?

Or is any movement
an improvement from standing still?

PIECES OF ME

I will not break apart.
I will not crumble.
I refuse to give away all of me.

I am no longer afraid of what
someone else will do with me.
I am more afraid
of what I will do without me.

I have lost myself to lonely souls.
To empty hearts so eager to be full
that they stole the life from
within me.

I will give away pieces;
this world will get nothing more
than a taste of my soul.
And I make no
apologies if I ever ask
for them back.

MOUNTAINS

I am made of mountains.
Curves of the earth.
My plains are not flat.
Nor simple.
Neither is my story.

For years I have
hidden behind layers.
Shields.
An attempt to hide
from the world.

> But these lines spell out a truth.
> My truth.

Every inch, every curve is a
reminder of my story.
I am learning that they
are all I need
to keep growing.

UNDER CONSTRUCTION

I feel as if I should constantly be
wearing a sign that says
"under construction".
I am forever changing my mind,
changing direction.
Some days, up seems down.
And tomorrow feels like
it has already happened.

I can't seem to make sense of
the pieces in front of me.
And so I set my own path.
I can see the road that so many others
have taken and I know
that it is not for me.

Does that make me better?
Does that make them better?

No, neither.
I bleed the same way you do,
but our breaths are not in sync.
I know that there is music playing
in your mind,
just as there is in mine.
But our tempos will never meet.

We walk, we talk,
and we continue
on our way as we venture
out into the wild ahead.

Your path, in my eyes,
paved with streets of gold.
Mine, well, mine are littered
with eyes of green.
Envious of all you have figured out
and sickened by all I have left
to learn.

But I keep walking.

Feeling lost in a world of u-turns.
Black and white in a world of color.

Someday soon I will find balance.
Someday soon I will find the answer.

TIME

Slow down time.
Let's take it easy.
Sleep, if you must.
But do not worry about bringing
tomorrow to me.

Let me have this moment.
And the next to cherish.

The hours slip
through my fingers
and holding on is
no longer an option.

I am not waiting
for you to give me
anything.

I am just asking you
not to take anything else away.

PILLOW TALK

I am frozen; drowning in a sea
of down blankets and oversized pillows.

Staring at the ceiling,
making shapes out of the white noise
above.

> Popcorn animals.
> Popcorn faces.
> Popcorn dreams.

I stare until I find myself.
Hidden within the white abyss.
Not exactly floating,
but not standing either.

> Just existing.

The waves of silence crash over me.
And wake me from my
momentary escape.

I am brought back to life.

Well, back to a reality at least.

BATTLE

I feel the weight of the battles
that wage between
my mind and my heart.
I feel the echoes
of lost tears dancing,
no, pounding upon my chest.

Thump. Thump. Thump.

There are no screams
of defeat.
No battle cries
signaling a war won.
There are no real winners.

One will always
feel a little empty.
But I have learned
to accept the brokenness
that is left behind.

I have learned that some days,
the path will be laid out.
Clear. Clean.

And then there will be days
where seeing five minutes ahead

will be too much to ask.

But eventually, the war will end.
My eyes won't be muddy with tears
and my soul won't be burdened
with questions.
I will breathe easy, if even only for
a minute.

.

OK

I am struggling.
I want my voice to be heard
but I am often afraid of the voices
that might answer back.

I want the world to
hear my song.
But I am so fearful
that the only noise I will make,
will be out of tune.

I watch the world move by.
It is mighty and fierce.
It is everything
that I dream to be.
Everything that I fear I am not.

Do I imitate what I see?
Fall into the mold that I know
will push me
to where I wish to be?
Or do I stay honest
and true?

HONEYSUCKLE AND FORGIVENESS

Walking between the
lines I have set out for myself.
I know this path will get me there.
I know that in this moment,
I am where I need to be.

But deep down, there is a voice
that is telling me to change my ways.

Move faster. Push harder. Dream bigger.

I am struggling to keep up.
I am struggling to stay true.
I am struggling,
but as long as I stay honest,
it is OK.

SILENCE

Have I committed to
standing in silence?
Did I do this to myself?
Or did I ever really have a choice?

Did my mouth
devour the words
before they left my lips?
Or did I even have
a chance to taste them?

I don't need to fill my soul with
unwanted stories or
edited dreams.

I don't need to hold on
to lines that I no longer allow
to direct me where to go.

I will clench my fist around all
that clouds my mind.
Gripping onto the idea
of letting go.
Irony at its finest,
but at least I will be able
to sleep at night.

BUT

I am learning to become
my original self,
in a world that so desperately wants
me to be anything but authentic.

I will hold tightly to the pieces that
my soul has grown to love.
And hold even tighter to the pieces
I have been trying to hide.

They make me stronger.
They make me, me.
They make me.

MADNESS

I crave the sweat
trickling down my back.
The stinky nonsense
of it all.
Losing myself to the heat.
Surrendering and giving
myself away to all
that shakes me from within.

I can't control my madness
any more than
the sun controls the sea.

It comes and it goes
as it pleases
and never looks back.

It doesn't care
who it pulls under.
Just that it
has something
beneath it to crash over.

I don't need all of those theatrics.
I am not that sadistic.

I don't need to pull you under
with me.

I just need to know that there is
ground beneath me
before I take another step
overboard.

MESSY

I know my soul needs watering.
A gentle hand, a tender voice.
It needs to be so consumed
with love, that there is no room
for anything else to enter it.

I need to douse it
with praise, and not
the kind that is seen only
through filters and dreams.
I need to love it, all of it,
with the intention of never asking
it to be anything other than
what it is.

I know this is what I need
to do.

But, I have been known to do
the opposite.
When life gets a little ugly,
I throw hate when I should
throw love.

I speak anger when I should let
compassion spill from my lips.

No, not with the world,
but with myself.
It is easier to show
forgiveness when I see the faults
of others.

Bu the faults raging in my reflection
scream too loud to be ignored.

Too loud to be forgiven.
Until now.
I will love myself.
I will be kind to my tender soul.

> *I will make no apologies for loving myself
> a little harder when life gets messy.*

THUNDER

I can't sleep.
The storm brews above my head
and I am lost in the thunder
that calls to me.

Have I let chaos rain in my heart?

No, I am not asking if chaos
reigns over my soul.
Causing destruction within my
very being.
I want to know if there is
a constant storm inside me.

Does it flood the cavities
and drown my every waking dream?
Or is a tamed chaos?

Do I tell it when to turn left
and when to die down?
Letting the adrenaline
flood my system just long enough
to wake me up?

Or, do I sleep through this storm?
Ignoring the rain as it washes me away.

WILD

I have broken free
from the chains I once
lived in.
My wrists are no longer bound
by the weight of my past.

I can taste my freedom
and I have only myself
to stop me.

I am free. Uninhibited.
I am unchained,
but I haven't lost sight of myself.

I am wild,
but you will never see me
running without purpose.

TAMED

I want to grow.
So why do I shrink myself down?
I face the world ahead of me
with arms wide open.
I am fearless until I'm not.

I hold power inside of me.
Like a storm carrying the thunder.
This monstrous sound echoes
from within.
Why do I try to wrap it
up in a tiny package?
Why do I try to build walls
that I know can't contain my power?

Brick by brick,
I can feel myself crumbling down.
The less I allow myself to be,
the less I will be.

And somehow, I have become
OK with that.

But this storm lives in a sky
that has no limits.

The lightning flashes and I can see it
stretch across the earth.

This soul was not meant to be tamed.

And so, I unravel this straight jacket.
I pull the string and my heart
bleeds open.

Free of the walls I had tried to build.
Free of the lies I had so desperately
tried to believe.

BROKEN

I am rearranging
all of the brokenness
until something beautiful
breaks through.

Because that's what we do, right?

Life isn't going our way,
we scramble together
all the broken pieces.
We collect all the "rubble"
and decide what is worth saving.

We toss aside, *(hopefully)*
the ugliness that no longer
belongs and we try
to make sense of the pieces
that are left over.

Sometimes,
things work out.
Sometimes.
the pieces stack neatly
side by side.

And then,
there are times when nothing
wants to fit.
No matter how perfectly
they should match up,
they refuse.

We break down
once again and rebuild.

We constantly tear and build.
Tear and build.
And, if we are lucky,
we find time somewhere in the chaos
to breathe.

STORMS

I am a silent storm.
Raging only in the night,
when the lights are low
and my pain is asleep.

I bring enough rain to
drown my own sorrows.

And lightening bright enough
to shed light on all that
I have fought so hard to forget.

I get lost in the darkness,
but I carry on.
The thunder backing
every step that I take.
Echoing outside
the walls of my heart.

Boom *(boom)* Boom *(boom)* Boom *(boom)*

I am a silent storm,
but a storm I will always be.

QUIET

There are moments I try
to quiet my soul.
Not to give it peace or rest.
No, to try to hide it away
from my mind.
Stronger than my heart
and my brain combined,
my soul leads me down the path
that I need to go.
But I let my fears out rank it.
My anger and my hurt
too often win the fight.

But this soul of mine will not cower.

It may hide for a moment;
step into the shadows to let me be.
But it always emerges.
Stronger than ever.
And often without speaking a word
louder than before.

FOOTING

My insecurities are eating away at me.
And while I might not be dead,
I am not exactly alive.

They step on my shadow.
I stumble.
I am so out of focus,
I don't even know where to land.
But, even in this state
of darkness and confusion,
I know this... I will land.
I always do.

My steps are getting longer.
My stride, shorter.
I am off balance,
but will soon find my footing.
I just need to keep putting
one foot in front of the other.

And soon enough,
I will be walking free.

SWIM

Some days,
I get stuck in my head.
I swim around without really looking
for a way out.
I let my heels dig into the roots of my soul.
I become grounded in everything
that has made me.

I stand frozen. Unmovable.

I will not shake when the wind
blows my way.
I will not fall when the storm
crashes through.

I am strong even when I am in hiding.

I find strength in the darkness;
in the questions.
I turn my anxious heart into a beat
I want to dance to.
And I give myself the freedom to
move when I am finally ready.

SOMETHING

I am not going to promise
that I will be *everything*.
At this point,
I can barely say that
I will be *something*.

But, I can promise to be me.

Every line.
Every inch of skin will be mine.
And I will wear it everyday.

Head held high.
I won't hide myself
because you are afraid
of what you see.

CARELESS

I am some kind of something.
I am just not exactly sure what yet.

I know that the secret lies
inside me.
Buried somewhere deep
within my bones.
Soaring through the marrow.

I will find it if I dig deep enough.

Break through the cavity
and let it bleed out.
I'll find it if i care enough to look.
In this moment, I am careless.

I am studying the lines
that are drawing my intentions,
and no longer fighting
to stay within them.

I see me as I am.

Something other than nothing.
I am just not exactly sure
what that means yet.

BREEZE

I am a breeze
on a silent night.
An echo in a room
without walls.

I am a sudden shift in the stars,
and a statue that has never
been sculpted.

I am a taste of something
yet to come,
and a memory
that has already faded.

I am.

I am,

I am.

PATH

I let myself fall into tomorrow.
Eyes wide open or shut;
at this point,
it doesn't matter anymore.

I will fall without looking back.
I will let my feet kiss the ground
before looking for another path
to travel.

POSSIBLE

I never knew it was possible
to lose yourself and find yourself
all in the same moment.

But here I am,
letting go of what
has been holding me down.

I am finally making room
for what will help me fly.

PLANS

I make plans only to have
lightening crash down
before the rain.

Without warning,
life happens.
and I get lost in the storm.

STUCK

A storm rages inside my heart
and gets lost in the chambers.
Never reaching
outside the walls that house it.

I've been silenced. Shut down.

I cast a shadow over
my own heart
with no intention of ever
seeking light.

I am midnight
trapped in a bottle.
A sandstorm caught
in the rain.

I am forever stuck in a moment.
Searching for something
that has already left me.

My voice is gone
and I am left with the taste of
yesterday on my lips.

I open my mouth to speak,
but only air passes over
my tongue.
I breathe deep.

One.

Two.

Three breaths.

I fill my lungs and pray I find
my voice again.
Until then,
I will live in the silence.
It speaks louder than my heart ever did.

PLUCKED

I am not a rose.
I will not be plucked
from the earth
only to die as the world
watches my beauty
fade away.
I am a wildflower.

I bloom
where I am planted.
And I have
planted myself where I am *free.*

CELEBRATE

Today I celebrate me.

I celebrate myself AS I AM.

Not who I wish I could be.
Not who I am working on becoming,
I celebrate who I am in this moment.

I celebrate the moments
I find beauty when the world
feels like it's against me.
I forgive myself for the moments
that I can't find any.

I will honor and praise what makes me
different.
Celebrate the uniqueness
that is coursing through my veins.
And promise to never again
hide it from the world
or myself.

RECALL

I don't recall the moment
that I stopped reaching
for someone else inside me.
The earth didn't shatter.
I wasn't suddenly numb
to the world
and all it threw at me.
It just happened.

One day I was reaching,
no, I was desperately
grasping for something,
anything alive within me.
Anything with a pulse
that didn't breathe my name.

And then the next, I was still.
There was no
sudden movement of desperation.
No jolt of lightning
that was keeping me
awake at night.
Striking my heart with the
footsteps of everything I imagined
I was lacking.

I don't recall the moment
I stopped reaching
for someone else inside me.

But, I don't recall the moment
I started either.

LAYERS

Is there really beauty
to be found in the broken?
Better yet, are we ever
really broken?

Do we die down?
Or do we just simply
chip away a little at a time?

We are made of layers.
Of yesterday's and of tomorrow's.
And even when we lose a layer,
there are still so many
that remain.

We may think that
we are falling apart.
Losing ourself along the way.
But, there is
so much more
to us than we remember.

So much more than we think
we can be.

So while I might feel
as though I am falling apart
or chipping away at what is,

I remind myself to look for what will be.

The uncovered layers.
The light in the cracks.
The paint beneath.

GENTLE

Be gentle with your soul.
Even storms have moments
of weakness.

Even the dessert gets thirsty.

Even the sleepless lose the fight
with the moonlight.

Be gentle.
Be gentle.
Be...

HORIZON

What happens when heartache
no longer wants to carry pain?
Does it toss it aside?
Only to be collected in the wind.
Like the dust in a breeze.
Is that where nightmares are born?

Or does it collect
all the tears and emptiness?
Bottle them up and throw them
to the flame.

Does it watch each memory
turn to ash?
Collecting the remains
and toss them out to sea.

Does it go down with the ship?
Or sail off into the sunset?

Does heartache
survive when
there is no pain to be found?
Or does it simply fade away
into the horizon?

DEEP WATERS

I fall to pieces
and just as quickly,
I put myself back together
again.
I am the thunder that shakes
my own soul
and the glue that mends me.

I bottle up the storm
until the glass begins to break.
Tiny cracks stem
from the bottom up.
Echoing in my mind,
as if I needed
one more reminder
of the rain ahead.

I swim
in the deep waters
that are flooding my soul.

I once thought the waves
would pull me under.

Treading water
was my idea of survival.

All these years,
I've been trying to escape
the inevitable.
I've tried to lose it along the way.
But no matter
how fast I run or how hard I swim,

the madness I carry with me
is here to stay.

WOMAN

I am a woman. Is that enough?
I have birthed new life
and watched life pass.
I give love when I am
almost empty.
And often refuse
what I need to survive.

I am a woman.
I have cradled more than
one weeping soul.
Refused to let
the daylight win,
when all I really wanted
was the night sky.

I walk in front,
not to lead, but to take on
the storm first.

I am a woman.
I haven given my best
only to receive the bottom
of the barrel in return.

HONEYSUCKLE AND FORGIVENESS

I have watched happiness
dance in other eyes,
as mine filled with tears.
I wake each day
ready to refuse defeat,
even when I feel as if I have
already lost the fight.

I am a woman.
And somehow, the world
still asks more of me.
The limits and lines
I draw don't seem to matter.

More. More. More.

This world will continue to take more.
Ask more.
Demand more.
And so now,
I can't help but wonder...
is it enough to say that I am a woman?

Or must I still give just a little bit more?

LIGHT

I don't recognize myself.
This body.
This "temple".

When did I become the owner
of something I feared?
When did I let the lines
that define my body, define my soul?

I hesitate when passing a mirror.
Will I find strength in all that I am?
Or will I once again walk briskly?
Avoiding eye contact at all costs?

It is a war, this struggle in my mind.
I am finally starting to
see the beauty from within.

Soon, I will stop searching
for shadows to hide behind
and instead see the light.

MOVEMENT

I will not be defined by the
curve of my hips,
but the movement
of my soul.

I will not judge
the pace of my steps.
Instead,
I will celebrate the distance
that I have traveled.

I will not be afraid of tomorrow,
just because yesterday
robbed me of pieces
of my soul.

THIRST

I find myself giving into the world.
No, not into what I think
it can hand me,
But what I think it
wants from me.

I let it slowly chip away
a little bit at a time,
the person that I want to be.
I don't measure up
to its standards.
I don't fit inside the mold
laid out in front of me.
I have stopped coloring
inside lines ahead of me.

Some days. I feel as if I am a book
that no one wants to read.

But, I continue to write the pages.
I fill them out with my story.
The story that no one else seems
to understand.
It's as if I'm speaking my own language.

But I find beauty in that.
I find beauty in the fact
that I've yet to change my voice.
Beauty in the fact
that I don't fit inside a mold.
I find beauty in needing only what
my soul craves to be happy.

I don't grab for more
than what will fit in my heart.
I don't thirst for more than what I need
to fill up my soul.

SURVIVAL

I don't pretend
that the answers live within me.
They don't dwell
inside as if they have laid
down roots.
Planted themselves
within my walls
and call me home.

I struggle to know the difference
between the paths in front of me.

But they often look the same.
My mind plays tricks on me.

Controlled chaos?

Not by choice.

Sometimes I lose myself
in the madness.

Sometimes I call it survival.

YESTERDAY

These weights are heavy,
and this life,
is so very long.
I walk forward.
One foot in front of the other.

I pause only to catch my breath.
Never looking back.
I have fallen down that hole
too many times.
There is no way I will be able
to climb back out.

I yearn for a tomorrow
that isn't laced with the pain
of yesterday.

I pray for a yesterday
that stays in the past.

RENEW

I have yet to see
a day that didn't begin
with the sun kissing the sky.

Somehow,
even the darkest
of nights wake to new light.
And if something
as majestic as the night sky
can renew each day,
than so can I.

STRONGER

I struggle with loving
the walls that contain me.
I either stare too long,
or I don't look at all.
I avoid mirrors and run
from anything that carries a lens.

If I don't see it, maybe it is not real.

I have beaten my soul down.
Torn it apart for being anything
other than what I've been told
to become.

But these walls are mine.
They protect the fortress
that is my heart.
I can no longer carry the weight
of the worlds judgment.

I am stronger than the world wants
me to be.

I am stronger than I believe.

ARMOR

I wish I were stronger.
That I wore a coat of armor
that covered my soul.

Keeping the words
from seeping in and
becoming a part of me.
I wish that I could stop
the tears.
Dead in their tracks.
Never letting them fall to begin with.

But, this coat of armor,
this "protector",
would it steal from me
more than it
helped me?

Would it keep
me from feeling
the warmth of my own skin?
Denying me of the beauty
of loving my own body?

Would it keep me from
taking breaths?
Stopping me from speaking
my truth?
Would I be able to string together
words if I never let
them touch me?

If I banished my tears,
would I know how it felt to
water my own soul?

THE CHASE

I spent yesterday chasing down
the day before.
Running after memories others
had dropped along the way.
I ran.
I ran as fast as I could
to collect them.
To keep them from becoming
one with the earth.
I prayed that someday,
they would be missed.

And so I held on to them.
Buried them deep in my pockets.
Locked them away for a day
with enough rain to remind the
world of how dry it would become
without me.

But that was yesterday.
Today, I am running after myself.
Circling the globe
to find answers
to the questions
that I am asking.

I chase after the light
that keeps me going.
It's always one step ahead.

Just far enough for me to keep reaching,
and close enough for me to taste.
I have planted my memories.
Buried them so deep
below the surface
that by the time they sprout above the earth,
I will be gone.

I couldn't toss them aside.
Send them away only to be forgotten.
No, they deserved a proper burial.
They died with my pain
and there will be no resurrection.

A part of me has left with them.
But I have finally seen the brilliance
in walking alone.
One set of foot prints
has never looked so tempting.
There is no confusion in my path.
No questions lingering behind.
Just empty shoulders and a heart full of hope.

CURVES

I am not the woman
I used to be.
And I am finally coming
to terms with that.
I use the baggage that I carry
to fight the demons.

They haunt me at night.
But I am slowly winning them over.
And while I know that there is
so much more that I can be,
I am slowly beginning to see
the beauty in everything
I have so desperately tried to hide.

PIECES

I have swallowed myself whole.
Perhaps, it was out of necessity.
Maybe, it was just fear.
This life has been a long one.
Fewer years than memories,
but still feeling as though
an eternity has passed.

I bend. I break. I falter.

And slowly attempt
to reconnect the pieces.
Some days, I feel as though
I am almost healed.

Other days, well, I bandage my soul
as best as I know how.
And I pray to my God
that I don't lose pieces of myself
along the way.

URGES

Chipped nail polish
and red lights.
The sun beats down on me.
Just another way for
the universe to rush
and push me forward.

"Move ahead", it yells at me.

There is no slowing down.
There is no pause.
I must walk forward.
I must push through.

I will keep treading water
until the urge to swim
is greater than
the urge to sink.

OWNERSHIP

This world acts as if
it owns me.
No, no hands are placed upon me.
I feel no unwanted touch.

But the words being spit
in my face seem to claim ownership.

> *"Shrink down to be loved."*
> *"Don't speak too loud if you want*
> *me to listen"*
> *"Stand tall, but not too tall."*

But I am not one for this world.
I will not give in to the ugliness
laid out before me.

I am fighting a war.
I am fighting to become myself
in a world that wants me
to be everything but.

DANCE

Some days I find myself
trapped behind closed doors.
I shut myself in.
Hide behind the walls
that I have built, and sway.

The music may have changed,
but, I celebrate the fact
that it is *still here.*

I won't hide behind my sadness.
We will dance until we both
grow tired.

SUNSET

I used to fear the sunset.
I was afraid of what I would miss
after the sun went down.

But I am learning
that there is a great deal of beauty
that can only be found in the quiet spots.
In the corners where
color and shapes do not exist.

In the darkness, where only echoes
and soft whispers can be found.
I won't deny the beauty
found beneath the yellow
that kisses the sky.

But I will celebrate all that I can find
within the silent abyss; my darkness.

TEMPLES

My body is soft.
Made of curves
that do more than twist and bend,
Always bringing the traveler back
to where he first started.

I never claimed to be
a temple made for worship.
I never thought that I carried
the weight of eyes filled with green,
except my own.

I bathe in the jealousy of all
we have been taught to worship.
I know that these
walls are far from the
temple I chase in my dreams.

But they are my walls.

Built out of all that's behind me
and everything I dream them to be.

ENOUGH

I am enough.
I am more than enough.
But I have learned
that when I start
craving more,
the only place to look
is within.

GRIP

I tighten my grip around everything
that I *truly* hold dear.
To everything
that has escaped my mind.
To the moonlight I find myself
dancing beneath.

I tighten my grip around all
that I fear I will someday lose.

I tighten my grip around myself.

I will never again hold on
to another soul harder
than I hold on to my own.

CHAOS

I am nothing less than self contained chaos.
I carry dreams
that have yet to be realized
and nightmares that I have tried to erase.

I watch the road behind me disappear.
Only to face forward
with my eyes shut.
I am tempted by jealousy.
Give into all that I wish I could be.
But I am swallowed by the thought
of never getting there.

I am a storm in a bottle.
An ocean in a bowl.
I spill.
Overflow.

There is too much of me
and at the same time,
there is not enough.
I am dreaming
and mindless in the same moment.

I am.
I am.
I am still more.

STRIDE

I own this body.
There is no one else in this world
who can stake claim to it.

There have been bidders.
There have been those
who felt it was their right
to let me know
which way they thought
that I should walk
and how long
my stride should be.

They follow me around
as if they were
stitched to my shadow.
Only disappearing
when the lights are out.

They fade into the sunset
only to rise with the morning sun.

Refreshed.
Renewed.

But, I do the same.
And once more,
I will make it my mission
to walk on.
Even if the weights of their whispers
make my steps a little heavier.

I will always walk on.

HONEYSUCKLE AND FORGIVENESS

Dear world,
I take it back. I take back every breath that I
gave away to those who were so very undeserving.
I take back every last one. I take back the silence
that I stood frozen inside of when my soul needed
to scream.

I take back the moments I coward in fear.
Afraid of what the steps ahead of me
might hold. I take each one back.
I take back the emptiness I gave away,
fearful that having nothing was somehow worse
than living with ugliness.

I take back every instance when I
was anything but myself.

I take back every apology for being true
to who I am.
I take it all back.
And I would like to formally (un)apologize for doing
so.

Forever true,
jessie michelle

ACKNOWLEDGMENTS

My beautiful/wild/tender-hearted/creative/ex-hausting/empowering/perfectly-imperfect chil-dren, each day I see in your eyes the woman that I hope to be. You look at me (most days) as if I am everything you need; as if I have yet to fail you. And while there are many moments I feel like this is the farthest thing from the truth, your love gives me the hope that I can someday be the mom I know you deserve. You three are my light and my reason for waking each morning.

Wade, this book is about loving yourself without needing the love of someone else. It is about find-ing strength in your core, and knowing that you can survive on your own, without another hand to hold. And even as I wrote each piece, knowing that this book would *not* be about romantic love, my mind would still travel to you. A little piece of you is laced into everything that I write. My dreams for us, and my darkest fears. You have supported my dreams and continue to support my heart with your own (even when I question it a million times). I am beyond blessed to walk this life with you at my side and in my heart.

My sisters, growing up with 4 best friends (alter-nating and at different times depending on life), was one of the biggest blessings. I am constantly learning more about myself by watching you all learn about yourselves. Even in the moments we aren't talking, or we are fighting with each other, I forever feel so blessed that I can call you sisters. Thank you for being strong women who fight for what their soul believes. Thank you for standing tall and showing my girls what it means to be a strong voice in a world that often still tries to quiet our tongues.

Dangie, thank you for lending your artwork to this book. From our days of glitter and vodka, you have been one of my biggest supporters when it comes to my writing. Thank you for always being there and not only listening to my craziness but giving me advice (future Dangie) when I had no idea which way to turn.

Cheri, thank you for lending your eyes to this book. For taking the time to read through the pages and giving me direction on which way to go. Moreover, thank you so much for showing the girls that following your dreams is so important. With four sisters, I never thought I would need/want for another, but I am so thankful to call you family.

HONEYSUCKLE AND FORGIVENESS

ABOUT THE AUTHOR

Jessie Michelle was born in Virginia and spent her early childhood living in Hawaii and then in Florida. She currently lives in Georgia with her husband and three children.

This is her second published work and she is currently working on her third book of poetry. She is a self proclaimed addict of love and coffee. She firmly believes that a little of each, (mainly love) will solve and heal almost all things. She writes about many facets in life, including love, heartbreak and body positivity.

You can find her work on Facebook, Instagram and online.

JESSIE MICHELLE

45052472R00075